STEP
BACK

STEP BACK

A Stepmother's Handbook

Margit Eva Bernard

Cotsen Occasional Press

Los Angeles

The Step Back philosophy is a simple concept for a strategy that requires regular practice to master—and the rewards are well worth the effort.

Stepping back prevents you from contributing to disorder. It allows you to be an observer, opening your field of vision to every aspect of the matter at hand, broadening your perspective and clarifying your judgement.

When you can see the issue from every angle, your awareness is enhanced. You develop a fresh interpretation of the situation. Now, instead of an impulsive *reaction*, you choose a thoughtful *action*.

Your feelings shift, your emotions are in check. You no longer become entangled in the confused energies of the moment. Your composure changes the prevailing condition—if only for yourself.

When you step back, you move forward on your own path to liberation.

CONTENTS

EDITOR'S PREFACE

first met Margit Bernard through a mutual friend, who told me Margit was looking for a writer to help create an heirloom memoir, intended as a gift from her husband to his grandchildren. At our first lunch, we immediately recognized a comfort level between us; she invited me to meet her husband, to see if he and I would find a similar rapport. After we shared a delightful dinner, they decided to move forward with me on the project.

During the months we spent producing the memoir, Margit occasionally spoke to me of a book she'd been working on for a few years, and asked if I'd cast my editorial eye on her notes. I already enjoyed working with Margit. The fact that her book was about stepmotherhood, and she wanted it to be an unvarnished portrayal, captivated me. I had my own perspective on the subject: I'd been a stepmother for 16 years.

It isn't terribly difficult to find an editor with a command of the language; it's a bigger challenge to find an editor who hears the writer's heart. Margit felt she'd found in me more than someone who'd organize her ideas and check her grammar. Because we are like-minded about many aspects of life, our ability to finish each others' thoughts regarding relationships, spirituality, marriage, and parenting made our work together enjoyable, almost effortless. Although she has a decidedly European voice, I knew Margit's theories would be familiar to any woman in any part of the world who has married a man with children, and it was my job to make her ideas readily accessible.

While working on Margit's book, it was inevitable that I'd find myself wandering through memories of my own time as a young stepmother. I remember being in a continual struggle to find a balance between the little joys and the enormous challenges, at a point in my life when informed stepmothering advice was nonexistent. What would I have given to be supported by at least one other person whose own experience could guide me—or, at the very least, comfort me? I wish I'd known a woman like Margit when I was 25.

It is always a pleasure to work with a person whose integrity is intact, whose confidence in her understanding is unqualified. Margit's candor about her own experiences as a stepmother, with her realistic clarity of hindsight, her search for a balance between heart, mind and soul, and especially her enthusiastic desire to help her fellow stepmothers find each other and support each other, comprise the core of her value. These attributes are precisely what I needed in an advisor when I embarked on my journey as a stepparent. Margit shines a bright light on the road, helps us recognize the pitfalls, suggests course corrections designed to protect the woman first, then the wife, then the stepmother, helping us to be more informed and better prepared stepmothers.

My mother recently referred to Margit as "the godmother of stepmothers" and, after 50 years in the role, she has unquestionably earned that moniker. I needed Margit when I was a stepmother. You may very well need her as much as I did. Fortunately, you now have her wit and her wisdom as your guide.

ALEXANDRA BARNES LEH
Los Angeles, California

FOREWORD

Wisdom comes in many forms.

Sometimes, a book about a highly specific subject—such as the experience of being a stepmother—proves to be a much broader and deeper discussion of life, love, and grace. A book full of inspiration for anyone who is lucky enough to read it. A book that deserves to be widely shared and treasured.

This is such a book. Margit Bernard describes her 50-year journey as a stepmother, always honestly and vividly. Like a master weaver, she includes many threads of contrasting colors and textures—painful truths, deep compassion, growing self-awareness, profound love, delightful wit, and enduring wisdom. The result is a tapestry that enriches all of our lives.

As a man and the father of five children, it's a safe bet that I will never get to be a stepmother. But this book gave me a much deeper appreciation for the experience of anyone who finds herself in that role. More than that, because this book is written so compellingly, I am a better person—a more aware and caring human being—for having read it.

This book, in sum, is an invitation to step back—to gain new perspective, feel greater compassion, and view life more fully. And in doing so . . . we are also encouraged to step forward. To open ourselves to the struggles and challenges of relationships—and to the lasting beauty and magic of sharing our lives with others.

In her final chapter, Margit Bernard asks us to consider this question: What's *your* story? That is an empowering question. It reminds us that every person has a valuable story to tell. And it also reminds us that every person can be the author of her own unique story.

As you read this marvelous book, you will feel enlightened as well as inspired. You will feel your heart opening wider with every turn of a page. And you will discover, as I did, that this is a book of authentic wisdom.

T. A. BARRON
Boulder, Colorado

INTRODUCTION

There are shelves full of books that promote healthy self-awareness and a marriage built on steadfast devotion—both of which are required for successful stepmothering. It's true in every aspect of life: your most important work is on yourself—simply because you have no control over others. But when you marry a man who has children from a previous marriage, you naturally feel there is much more to care for than your own marriage; even if you only see the children every other week, they play a recurring role in your life. Whatever plans you make are often, if not always, formulated with your husband's children in mind.

It's very likely you did not, or will not, marry a man for his children. Yet, if they are integral to your husband's life, you must immediately and automatically incorporate them into yours, from the moment you say, "I do."

It seems obvious that women in their 20s and 30s who marry fathers are also entering into a longterm relationship with the father's young children . . . and women in their 40s and 50s are choosing—however unwittingly—ongoing relationships with teenagers and twenty-somethings. The woman needs to seriously consider this before she becomes a bride. Love is the purest motivation for marriage; but an acknowledgement and acceptance of the day-to-day reality is a critical component in the success of any marriage—especially that which includes a preexisting family.

How does a woman prepare for this continuing challenge? Is there a mysterious formula, a special technique, an established method by which a woman can gracefully move into both roles—wife and stepmother—fully prepared for every pitfall?

Anyone who is, or has been, a stepmother, has a distinct point of view about the experience, usually laced with as much frustration as satisfaction. This sounds like every mother's experience, doesn't it? But the differences are striking. A stepmother's challenges and needs are similar to a birth mother's only in that she is an adult and they are children.

After two marriages, seven stepchildren, and with 50 years' worth of perspective, I wish to relate my rather unusual experience to those stepmothers who find themselves struggling . . . and to help prepare those women who are embarking on a new life as a stepmother.

The position I put forth is not bathed in flattering pink light; I offer my thoughts from a decidedly realistic side of the experience. But I feel it is vitally important to be realistic when considering a path so especially fraught with complications. It is difficult enough to navigate the murky waters of marriage; it is much more complicated to instantly include the husband's children in the mix!

I want to say this to every stepmother: take it a little easier, try not to be so insistent, try not to have your desires dominate—and not just with the stepchildren, but with your husband, your family, your friends. The moment you step back from whatever it is that exasperates you, you get an unrestricted view of the situation—and you can take a breath before you move forward.

We often need the kind of guidance and encouragement offered by those with deep hearts and clear vision, and Kahlil Gibran's extraordinary classic, *The Prophet*, has been just such an inspiration for me. The wisdom of Gibran's profound writings, and a few choice thoughts from other insightful philosophers, are woven throughout this book, asking us to see ourselves differently: not trapped in an impossible predicament, but as a valuable and adaptable part of the expansive panorama of life—a view we can only appreciate when we *step back*.

MARGIT E. BERNARD
Los Angeles, California

1

A Woman First

Motherhood is a biological, perhaps psychological, imperative for many women, even without society's persuasive expectations that women procreate. Men are not exempt from this assumption, and are also influenced by familial and societal pressures to have a family that includes children. Even if the couple can't produce their own offspring, there are children in the world who need and want to be cared for, and adoption is a loving, noble way to fulfill everyone's needs and desires.

But motherhood was never a primary part of my life plan; I simply wasn't maternal in that sense. All I truly wanted was to marry a good man and live a good life . . . and I was lucky enough to fulfill those wishes more than once. Twice, I fell in love with men who had good hearts and exceptional minds, and who lived productive, successful lives. Both times, I married them. Both times, I was tested at a level I had not consciously sought: I was given, and accepted, the inadvertent opportunity to experience motherhood—as a stepmother.

As a young woman, I had very specific ideas about the role a mother plays in her child's life. In my limited knowledge, I thought a stepmother essentially plays the same role in the lives of her stepchildren. Soon after I married my first husband, I discovered that one bears very little resemblance to the other!

In my first marriage, I inherited four stepchildren . . . in my second, I have three. I cannot say I was welcomed by any of my husbands' children; I cannot point to many days of familial joy. But, if I had not been presented with those challenges, I would never have learned as much about myself as a woman, and about life as a stepmother, as I know now.

—o—

I was born and raised in Czechoslovakia, by a mother and father whose approach to parenting was the result of their own upbringing. They came from a formal European culture, in which the relationship between parents and children was based on respect, and building appropriate boundaries—not merely driven by love and more love. In our home, disobedience was never without consequence.

Whenever my mother punished me, I'd think of the most horrible thing I could possibly say to her. The first time I thought of it, I was maybe 8 or 9, and being rebellious. It came to me so easily; I'd spit it out of my mouth, the worst of the curses I could hurl: "You're a . . . a *STEPMOTHER!*" My expression of contempt was, for her, like a hat that didn't fit—accordingly, it caused her no pain. Perhaps it even seemed absurd to her.

But *was* it absurd? The negative characterization of stepmothers was established long before I was born: motherhood is idealized and stepmotherhood is demonized. I was calling my mother a monster, a witch . . . so the stepmother moniker fit, as far as I was concerned.

Years later, when I became a stepmother, it never occurred to me that *I* was a stepmother. Certainly, if I *were* a stepmother, I wouldn't be evil!

The truth is, the only role I was prepared to play in my marriages was that of the woman—not the wife, or the stepmother, but the woman to her man. There may be those who consider this idea antiquated and anti-feminist, or exclusive of the LGBT community. While I do come from a generation that still clings to notions about men and women now deemed old-fashioned, I ask you to consider another perspective: referring to ourselves as women first is, in actuality, more authentic than automatically referring to ourselves as wives and mothers and stepmothers and godmothers. We are women first; we become these other things as a result of our choices in life. In a healthy male-female relationship, a good man wants a good woman . . . not a passive partner, but a compassionate companion; not the "better half," but the other half, the yin to his yang. I may be overstepping my breadth of knowledge here, but I believe the same can be said in gay and lesbian relationships, as we all carry within us male and female tendencies. Regardless of the bodies we inhabit, in some of us, the male is stronger; in some, the female. Our need for emotional balance can be met when we are in relationships with people whose natural disposition compliments our own.

Both of my husbands and I found this balance in our partnerships. But, because neither of them asked me to take the position of stepmother, I did not zero in on the role. After all, my first husband was divorced, so his children still had a living mother—and the children of my second husband, who had been widowed years before we met, were young adults. I had married these fathers without thinking about the effect of their fatherhood on our relationships.

It did not take long before I learned how their children would affect my marriages, and my life.

2

A Wife and a Stepmother

My first husband had recently gone through a divorce when we married. His first marriage lasted 26 years, and produced four children— three girls and one boy—who were 11, 16, 18 and 20 years of age when I officially became their stepmother at the age of 30. They'd come from a good, polite home. The children had no idea there were problems between their parents until the morning they were told a divorce was imminent. Their parents were careful to affirm their love for the children, and let them know that the breakup had nothing to do with them.

Their mother remarried first, and moved to a nearby town. I came into my first husband's life about a year later; he kept me a secret from the children until our wedding was announced (I think that, for a long time, he wasn't sure he wanted to get married again). The boy and girls received me courteously and respectfully. They knew I had not caused the breakup of their parents' marriage, and all was apparently well in our new arrangement.

The youngest lived with their mother and new stepfather; the older children were in college. As my first husband and I discussed our future together, he made it clear to me that he did not want to create a new family; if I wanted to have children, he was not the right man for me. So, I had to be honest with myself. Ultimately, I knew I wanted to be his wife more than I wanted to be a mother. It was then that I had my first thoughts about what it would mean to be a stepmother.

I came to the children with a big heart, ready to embrace all of them, eager to create a loving environment for my husband and his children. I believed my attitude was the best I could have . . . that it created every potential for good times and great harmony.

The first indication that I was wrong came when we bought a house; each child asked, "Where is *my* room?" We reasoned with them that the intimacy of one-to-one visits with each of them would be far more nourishing for each relationship. To that end, we always had one of them over for the weekend—especially the younger children. I made sure everything was as I thought it should be in the home, and my husband seemed content in his dual roles. Then, one of the children would come late to the table, or neglect to wash for dinner, or bring a newspaper to read (if this had been the era of smart phones and iPads, no doubt technology would have come to the table, too!).

I admit, I might have been a bit more forward about my expectations than they were accustomed to, but I thought nothing of asking (not demanding) that they come to the table on time, having washed their hands, and leave their reading material behind. I'd receive a "Sure, of course" response—but they'd invariably do as they pleased.

Surely, such small things need not be considered serious infractions—why should I have made a fuss? I have found that it is in the details of behavior that one learns the measure of another's hostility. I soon understood that these minor signs of ignorance were designed to let me know that my wishes were of no importance to them. What could I do about this show of disrespect from my new stepchildren?

I acted on my feelings. And I had to defend those actions, by saying that I was showing them how to be part of the team, with common courtesy. But I was a frustrated teacher; although what I asked of them was important to their daily lives, and offered with the best of intentions, it was not appreciated by the "principal"—my husband. One day, he said to me, loud and clear, "Look—when they come for a visit, I want to enjoy them for those one or two days, not be their disciplinarian!" My response: "You are the father, and you have a responsibility to guide them in their behavior!" He did *not* respond well to my admonishment, especially when I got more specific about his three daughters:"What kind of message are you sending to your girls? For the rest of their lives, they're going to look for somebody like their father . . . but their father doesn't exist, because you don't show your real face to them. You show the face of an uncle, who is totally accepting and totally supportive. I have nothing against that, but if something isn't right, you voice it, you don't just let it go."

After months of trying to make headway with the children in an assortment of ways, I became aware that I was losing sleep, losing the warm and loving interaction I once enjoyed with my husband, losing everything about my life I held dear. I was miserable. I dreaded visits from the children— especially when conversations between their father and me were regularly interrupted by the children.

Just one way in which they showed their disregard for me.

I felt less like a wife and stepmother and more like the housekeeper—making everything nice, cleaning up after them, taken for granted—and I was exhausted by my seemingly useless efforts.

When I finally let my husband know my feelings, he was dumbfounded; he was, he said, entirely unaware of all the slights and disrespectful behavior towards me. Then, he offered an unexpected opinion: "Maybe this is all too much for you. Maybe you want a divorce." Now, *I* was the one who was dumbfounded. "How can you think such a thing? This has nothing to do with you and me—this is about the relationship between your children and me." I explained that they had been trying (consciously or unconsciously) to get me out of their lives. I told my husband that what his children really wanted was to have their father all to themselves.

This had never occurred to my husband. He believed his children wanted him to be happy; they surely knew how much he loved me, and how happy I made him. I assured him, he was mistaken; children are not conscious of their parents' happiness.

He didn't understand that children—his, or anyone else's—are inherently self-centered and self-involved. They want what they want for their own comfort and well-being—and, in this case, I did not deliver that comfort to them.

I was fortunate that, once my husband heard my perspective, he was sensitive and psychologically astute enough to start paying attention, observing the myriad annoying behaviors against me. This shift in his understanding changed our marriage for the better. Our lives became much more enjoyable, and we stayed married for 24 years.

I was grateful that our relationship had been salvaged; but I had wanted to make a positive difference in the lives of my stepchildren, too. However, my European upbringing was not in keeping with the American fun-and-games, less-defined parental roles. What happened, I wondered, to honoring your father and mother? And (at the very least) showing respect to your stepmother?

I realize now that their behavior toward me was not a personal affront; they would likely have treated anyone in my position with the same disregard. But it was hurtful to me, and I began to shut down to them, which was not my natural state. Now, I understand that I had a deep-seated need to insert myself into the situation between the children and their father, to make a new situation between the children and me, to create a team of trusted, supportive members. However, the reality for my stepchildren was that I stood between them and their father. And they could not understand that their father's love for, and attention to, me had nothing to do with his love for them.

3

A Widow and a New Life

And then, my husband died.

I was heartbroken for every reason imaginable. Losing this dynamic, loving man, who had been my partner for almost a quarter-century, left me completely empty, and looking for comfort. One especially beautiful offering of condolence came from my four adult stepchildren who, as we all said goodbye to each other, promised me: "We'll always be here for you." A deeply touching tribute, I thought. But now, as I grieved for my husband, I felt irretrievably lost . . . which is naturally the place one must start in order to find one's self again.

I knew my life wasn't finished; I was too young— where should I look for the starting point in my next chapter? I was almost immediately drawn to India. I needed guidance, and I wouldn't find what I required in Beverly Hills. India was so far from the life I'd lived with my husband. It was the perfect place for my quest.

My husband died in late August; perhaps a month later, I flew to India. I was taken to see a guru, an Indian spiritual teacher with whom I desperately wanted to talk about my loss. Even before I spoke, the guru looked at me sternly and said, "Not one word about the past! The past is gone! It is finished!" This was not at all the exchange I'd hoped for.

As Christmas neared, I decided to go to a place in which I would not be reminded of the holiday my husband and I loved to celebrate. So, when I was invited to return to India for the wedding of friends, it seemed like a wonderful gift to me. And when the sister of the groom asked if I would like to meet her guru, I gratefully accepted.

It was the evening of December 24th. We rode in a taxi for two hours on a dark road, and the thought came to me, "Thank you, God, this is what I wanted, to be in a place that has nothing to do with Christmas."

We arrived at the ashram, and it was filled with Americans and Europeans offering their humble service to the charismatic spiritual teacher, Gurumayi. As I joined the line of devotees who were receiving the guru's blessing, I noticed that she would occasionally reach into a bucket, bring out a small stuffed toy—a dog, a bear, a doll—and throw it at certain people, who'd catch the toy and blush in ecstasy. Now, it was my turn to receive her benediction. She gazed at me for a long moment, reached into the bucket, and a small red thing streaked through the air, landing in my hands—I looked down to see that Gurumayi had tossed Santa Claus at me!

Again, I was taken aback. My search for spiritual solace had reaped one severe admonition and one stuffed Santa. I had no idea that these encounters were precisely the guidance I sought, the very recalibration I needed.

—o—

I was still in Delhi as the new year approached, and decided that I wanted to spend New Year's Eve alone. My friends argued with me, but I was adamant that I start the coming year on my own, and in an unfamiliar city: Bangkok. My friends reluctantly took me to the airport, and I waited for my flight in the lounge, quietly sobbing to myself. Through my sniffling, I heard a woman on the phone: "Look, you must get my makeup bag to me, a woman cannot be without her makeup!" I glanced at the short, blonde woman who was so frantic about her missing cosmetics, then returned to my private sorrow.

I arrived in Bangkok, and as I made my way to Customs, I saw her again. "Did you ever get your makeup bag?" She smiled and said, "Yes, I did. You can understand how important that was to me!" She introduced herself, and asked where I was staying. "This your first time in Bangkok, yes? We can share a taxi—taxi drivers here set their prices however they wish. The trip could cost you $20 or $200." It turned out we were staying at the same hotel, and on the cab ride, I let her in on the decision I'd made as a new widow, to celebrate New Year's Eve solo. "Well, that's a great idea, but you're not going to be alone, because I'm going to a function, and you're coming with me!"

This persuasive woman whose makeup bag was critical to her travels? She happened to be a friend of the Dalai Lama! That night, and every night of my stay in Bangkok, I was surrounded by all kinds of lovely people. Until I returned to Los Angeles, I was never alone.

The spiritual underpinnings of my life were gently exposed through these unexpected experiences. In the wake of profound loss, I had made choices that were designed to get what I thought I needed—and I ended up getting something very different, even better. When I let go of my desires and expectations—even just a little—I received exactly what I truly required.

—o—

My husband and I had a house in Santa Barbara, which I decided to sell after I returned to the States from my Asian journey. And I made up my mind to move to Paris—the idea of "poor widow Margit" was too much for me. I had no prospects, but found a job through the connection of friends, and established myself in this new life on my own. Little by little, I found my footing in the company, although some considered me a wealthy dilettante. They didn't know I'd had my own career before I married; they had no idea I had managed my own successful shop, and had solid business savvy. But I soon proved myself to my colleagues, and to myself.

—o—

I'd met the man who would become my next husband in America—a widower with three adult children—and returned to the States when we decided we belonged together. My second husband and I married shortly after I turned 60 . . . and we have been deeply devoted to each other ever since.

I've said that I have never been filled with the maternal drive; but, if it hadn't been too late, I would happily have had children with my second husband. We are fortunate that our partnership needed nothing more to make it complete.

He loved me because, as he said, "You are your own person." Buoyed by his respect for me as a woman and a human being, I felt empowered to be myself in every aspect of our marriage. He appreciated this. His children, however, did not—or, if they did, they did not make it apparent to me. It was a familiar dynamic, and I was the common denominator.

Because of my wholehearted love for my husband, I enjoyed creating situations in which he, his children and I came together as a family—I believed these pleasurable things could lead to a warmer togetherness. But none of it really took hold. Once again, it was difficult for me to understand that their disengagement had nothing to do with me. By the time I joined the clan, the daughters had their families, the son had his family. My efforts were incidental in their lives, and their indifference confounded me and made me sad. My husband would see that I was distressed by the lack of appreciation, and he'd say to me, "When are you going to stop?"

His relationship with his children was profoundly complicated by a tragedy that had befallen his family during his first marriage; he had years before I showed up to form his strategy with his children. Then, I came into his life with everything he loves about me, everything he longed for. And I was not only bringing that to him unreservedly, I was willing to share it with his children, as a natural extension of my love for him. But when he said to me, more than once, "When are you going to stop?" I now realize, this was his way of advising me to step back.

—o—

Both of my husbands were well-established in professions they loved. My first husband was an accomplished and passionate screenwriter and film producer; my second husband is a successful businessman, with a multitude of interests apart from his company. I wasn't filling any need in them, other than trust and unconditional love.

I went into my second marriage with the same thoughts and ideas I had in my first marriage; I still hadn't learned that the definition of insanity is doing the same thing over and over and expecting different results!

It took me two husbands and seven stepchildren to see that I could have prevented so much pain, had I known what I know now: that wishful thinking and a loving heart are not enough for a stepmother to bring to her new family. I was, like every stepmother, at the mercy of the way the children had been raised. And I had no one in my life to advise and guide me. Experience was my only teacher.

4

You are Not a Mother

"Your children are not your children.
They are the sons and daughters of Life's
    longing for itself.
They come through you but not from you,
And though they are with you yet they belong
    not to you.
You may give them your love but not your
    thoughts,
For they have their own thoughts.
You may house their bodies but not their souls,
For their souls dwell in the house of to-morrow,
    which you cannot visit,
not even in your dreams.
You may strive to be like them, but seek not to
    make them like you.
For life goes not backward nor tarries with
    yesterday.
You are the bows from which your children as
    living arrows are sent forth.
The archer sees the mark upon the path of the
    infinite,

and He bends you with His might that His
   arrows may go swift and far.
Let your bending in the Archer's hand be for
   gladness;
For even as He loves the arrow that flies, so He
   loves also the bow that is stable."

∾ KAHLIL GIBRAN, *THE PROPHET*

The decision to raise a child is as profound a choice as any responsibility a human being can make. Greater than the love between the couple, this is a love beyond them, a commitment deeper than marriage. It is generally easy to create a child; after that, the parental responsibilities are vast, and last a lifetime . . . but what if the marriage does not last as long?

Bringing an innocent, helpless, needy life into the world requires much of mere mortals. Yes, the human race has been recreating itself since the world began—but it's only in the last century that the burden of parenthood has become an acceptable excuse for the demise of a marriage. Children can bring much joy and satisfaction to a couple—if that couple is strong and secure in their commitment.

When a woman bears a child, she is giving life with her own body. Her role as the wife expands to an even greater role as the mother—sometimes, to the detriment of the marriage, if the man is unable to reconcile the inevitable changes this new being brings to the relationship.

Aside from the changing responsibilities to each other as a couple, the mother must endure hormonal shifts during her pregnancy . . . and, perhaps, a postpartum depression that the father will never experience. His work was done once his sperm found her ovum. Now, it's all on the mother . . . no matter how understanding he might be, his participation in this process is limited. He can take the Lamaze classes, stand by her side in the delivery room, hold her hand, help her breathe through the pain. But the pain itself is all hers . . . and it creates an ineluctable connection between the mother and the baby.

Because the traditional household is, from a practical standpoint, nearly non-existent these days, it is no longer true that the role of breadwinner belongs solely to the husband and father. But there is one aspect of the husband-wife relationship that is still heavily tested when children join the couple: many men have trouble accepting a diminishing sexual return once the home contains a child, and this dissatisfaction can lead to the end of the marriage.

What place does this information have in a discussion about stepfamilies? With the divorce rate in our current culture at an all-time high, it follows that more stepmothers, stepfathers, and stepchildren will be created. I am not alone in believing that looser definitions of commitment between two people have much to do with this phenomenon. A child will test any commitment made between the parents; only when that commitment is solid can the marriage survive.

A child must be wanted for itself, out of love—but when a couple chooses to have a baby, or more than one, to keep the marriage together, they have made a decision that disrespects the child before he or she is born.

—o—

Of course, the end of a marriage doesn't always come as the result of divorce. When death takes a woman from her family before the children have fully grown and created lives of their own, the heartbreak seems irreparable to all who suffer the loss. For the children, it is certainly a pain that cannot be alleviated by the appearance of a new woman in the father's life—and a potential stepmother in this context should know from the start that she will be competing with an ethereal being, a cherished ghost. Even if she was not the most nurturing mother while she lived, the mother will likely be lovingly enshrined in her children's hearts. The stepmother has to find ways to live in the shadow of that monument with respect, without resentment, and with a generous measure of deft poise that no birth mother is expected to display.

In the instance of divorce, it doesn't really matter who or what caused the breakup between your husband and his previous wife. The fact that there was a divorce automatically creates feelings of failure for everyone concerned. Your husband might ask himself, "Was there something I could have done to prevent it?" And your stepchildren might wonder, "Was it something I did that caused it?"

Any persuasion to the contrary on your part will be of little help, if any at all. A father's feelings of guilt are a kind of penance—and, ironically, indulgence in such wallowing can ultimately relieve the pressures of remorse. It is, however, difficult to watch your partner make incorrect decisions regarding the children while in the throes of self-reproach. He wants to please them, to relieve them of their own suffering, to make up for the love they seem to be missing as a result of the family's dissolution. When you point out this behavior to your partner, it fuels his negative feelings about himself—and suddenly, you're in the midst of your own disagreement with him.

No matter how close you and he are, you are not (nor will you ever be) as emotionally involved with his children as he is. This makes it easier for you to see how damaging his behavior is, and it's terribly hard not to voice your opinion the instant you see it. You want to point out the harm it can bring— to protect him, the children, and yourself. A guilty parent's permissiveness can cause a false sense of entitlement in any child; a condition that takes much time and effort to rectify.

—o—

Parenting is a difficult minefield to navigate under the best circumstances. But, when so many fissures were caused before you arrived, yours is not to set about repairing them. You must cultivate an unemotional response to your husband's more destructive choices, so that your own vision of the entire situation is unobstructed by feelings. When you take a step back, you have a more comprehensive view that allows you to see—then, in time, address—everyone's needs.

Diplomacy is difficult when emotions, and pre-conceived notions, are involved. A stepchild—and, for that matter, a husband—will, however sub-consciously, think you are operating in the interest of your own agenda. After all, you just got here; what makes you think you know how your hus-band should treat his children in the wake of an emotional, and physical, estrangement from their real mother? Parents often don't like to get advice from their own parents or siblings—how can you come in and impose your unsolicited recommendations on this broken family without being suspect?

I have noticed a prevailing belief among birth parents that they are best qualified to raise their children, under every circumstance. They seem to believe that they know their children as well as they know themselves. If parents were more open to informed input from experienced sources, instead of perpetuating their problems by isolating themselves and their children from a more inclusive outlook, their relationships might be more positive and productive. In this case, the stepmother (with her love for her husband, and her wish to create harmonious connections between every family member) can be of help.

But stepmothers face an enormous prejudice, fed in part by the misguided belief that "real" mothers and fathers know best. A patient and careful cultivation of trust is the only solution. Trust requires patience and more patience; this is, by far, the most challenging trait to master.

—o—

The children have not chosen you as their stepmother; they'd never want to do so. Any resentment you receive from them is a result of the breakdown of the original family structure—whether the mother has divorced their father, or died, makes little difference. You are seen as a replacement they never wanted. If you try, even in the most gentle way, to guide or admonish your stepchildren, you'll likely hear the retaliatory phrase (whether under their breath or at the top of their lungs), "You're not my mother!"

Your love is not important to them; it has no basis in their reality. They will try at every opportunity to diminish you, to remove you as the "obstacle" between them and their father. They may set up certain scenarios designed to make you fail, so they can be proven right in their assessment of you. One mistake on your part can have repercussions that last far longer than is reasonable.

They don't want to like you—you are an outsider, an interloper, a stranger in their own home. And, even if you came along years after the demise of their parents' marriage, they will subconsciously accuse you of having come between their mother and father. Their affection belongs to their mother, not to you.

In other relationships, you usually have some credits from past kindnesses, a cache of loving memories created, that mitigate any misstep you might make. But in the world of the stepchild, one wrong move, one slightly critical comment, erases instantly any goodwill you may have built. If you respond to this as any normal human being would—with an anger stoked by hurt feelings, for instance—the stepchild smears you with another layer of recrimination.

You want only to create win-win situations. There will be times when you think you've won and, in reality, you've lost.

It's easy to see how a well-intentioned stepmother might, out of such hurtful rejection, become the "stepwitch" famed in children's fantasies! It doesn't make sense in the real world; so, *you* must make an extra effort to make sense of it.

There is nothing you can do about their feelings—but there is much you can do to protect your own feelings, which may, in turn, set an example for the way your stepchildren ultimately respond to you.

Clearly, it is the stepmother's responsibility to establish some measure of trust between herself and her stepchildren if any form of love and respect are to follow. But how?

It is said we teach people how to treat us by the way we treat ourselves. Showing ourselves genuine love and respect, and showing others that you are trustworthy in word and deed, conceivably creates a model for your stepchildren (and, not incidentally, your husband) to honor and emulate.

And, you have to take each step one at a time.

5

The Steps to Take in Your Relationship with Yourself

Stepping back is a form of self-protection—which, in turn, creates more room for the stepchildren to be themselves, whoever they are. Given this opportunity, they might not turn out to be the kind of people you'd want to spend time with if they were not in your family.

But, it doesn't really matter . . . ultimately, you must do this for yourself. If you don't take steps on your own behalf, all your other steps will be incomplete.

BE TRUE TO WHO YOU ARE.

"Your hearts know in silence the secrets of the
    days and the nights.
But your ears thirst for the sound of your heart's
    knowledge.

> You would know in words that which you have
> always known in thought.
> You would touch with your fingers the naked
> body of your dreams. And it is well you
> should."
>
> ∾ KG

My first husband and I flew to New York for therapy with his son, now a young man who wanted a deeper understanding of his father and himself. When the conversation came around to his relationship with me, his son said to the therapist, "It was very difficult to get close to Margit, because she was always happy. I felt pain, and I could not confide in her because she was always happy."

The psychiatrist, who had already conferred with me about my childhood, explained to my stepson, "As a child, Margit was rewarded if she smiled and was joyous. This behavior earned her the attention of her mother or father . . . consequently, she took that as the thing to do in her life. You, very early in your life, found out that if you threw a tantrum, if you were down, miserable, made a face—you got attention, because everyone wanted to make you happy. You and Margit come from two very different ways of dealing with things."

I was sorry that it had taken so long for us to come to that understanding. But I was obviously glad I had not changed my demeanor to suit my stepson ... it would not have been true to who I am.

Be a good listener.

"The reality of the other person lies not in what he reveals to you, but what he cannot reveal to you. Therefore, if you would understand him, listen not to what he says, but rather to what he does not say."

ᐧ KG

You must set aside your need to give advice. A mother directs her child from the minute the baby opens his eyes; the same can be said when a woman takes seriously the role of stepmother. After all, you have more experience, you want to have a positive influence on the child, you have only the best intentions—but the habit of automatically telling your stepchild what to do prevents you from letting the child be heard. A young person has thoughts and feelings that deserve to be expressed; a child is a human being who needs to be understood. When we don't truly listen to children, it is a sign of disrespect.

It isn't easy, especially when you're not really interested in what the child has to say. There shouldn't be any shame in admitting it: a mother who spends 12 hours a day with her child will lose interest in the child's undeveloped ramblings, craving a 5-minute conversation with an adult, any adult, at the end of the day!

Almost every time I shop in a supermarket, I notice at least one mother's lack of respect for her child. She's shopping, consulting her list, often taking and making calls on her cell phone, while her child (whether seated in the shopping cart, or trailing behind) is making his or her desires known (sometimes, so everyone in the store can hear!). The mother (or perhaps a stepmother) is either acceding to the child's every wish or arguing against the demand. There's no moment of connection, no curiosity about the child's request, no indication that the mother is listening or the child is being heard.

—o—

I know that a mother is a juggler, a woman who deals with many competing interests, whether she's blissfully married to an exemplary man and has a house staff, or struggles as a working single mother of four. But the mother who is a yes-woman and the mother who always says no are the same: they are not listening to the person in their care. This indifference creates a dysfunctional pattern for the relationship between the adult and the child, and tends to set a poor example for the child's future relationships.

The same can be said for a stepmother, for different reasons—unless we have children of our own, or our stepchildren live with us, our lives are not enveloped in the day-to-day experience of motherhood, and the adjustment from adult to child can be an awkward effort. But when we stop— even for just for a moment—and step back from our own position, we can listen more attentively. Then, we have a better chance of hearing the child, connecting with them, understanding their desires, and addressing their needs.

Never try to take the "mother" role. There can be only one mother; you must always be mindful of that fact.

Most of the advice a stepmother gives a stepchild is unsolicited. Sometimes, it's an egotistical motivation: you want to show how you can be helpful, how you can manage things. You want to be seen and heard, not treated like a "non-person."

But there is a built-in resentment against you; you know you're being tested, and you want to show how capable you are—even if you weren't the one who gave birth to the child. You're in continuous competition with the mother; it doesn't matter if the mother is still physically present in the child's life or not. She exists in the children, and always will. The children will protect her because she is in their blood; they share genetics. You cannot compete with DNA.

"The more we witness our emotional reactions and understand how they work, the easier it is to refrain."

ॐ PEMA CHODRON

SMILE WITH SINCERITY; AVOID PHONY KISSES AND COMPLIMENTS.

"The privilege of a lifetime is to become who you truly are."

ॐ C. G. JUNG

Show your authentic self by exhibiting self-respect; this allows you to show respect to your stepchildren.

If you achieve a certain understanding and acceptance, your smile will naturally be genuine . . . and it
is more likely your stepchildren will respond in kind.
If you think about it, your stepchildren are, in actuality, critical to your self-development, giving you an
opportunity to become more than you already are.

PROJECT EASE AND CONFIDENCE IN YOUR
POSITION AS STEPMOTHER, BY DEVELOPING TRUST
IN YOUR OWN GOODNESS, YOUR OWN BETTER SELF.

When I think of my own childhood, and listen to
my friends who are mothers and stepmothers, I
often hear similar language—that of women who are
either repeating our mother's experiences, or push-
ing against them. Comparing our mothering to the
mothering we received may be common, but it isn't
fair to who we are as individuals, and it often shows
in how we project ourselves to others.

"You are the sky. Everything else—it's just the
weather."

∽ PEMA CHODRON

6

The Steps to Take in Your Relationship with Your Husband

KNOW WHY YOU ARE THERE.

"When love beckons to you, follow him,
Though his ways are hard and steep.
And when his wings enfold you yield to him,
Though the sword hidden among his pinions
    may wound you."

∾ KG

Examine your reasons for wanting to be in a partnership with this man—and be honest, because it isn't always about love alone. Perhaps it is a desire for security, or status, or children. These are understandable inclinations—but making such a commitment should be a sign of respect for your partner, if you wish to have a lasting and satisfying relationship. It is a promise you make to yourself, as well as to your husband . . . so, as long as your relationship with your husband is built on a foundation of love and respect, you have a better chance for success in the marriage. Love can soften many blows of misunderstanding between you and your partner . . . and, in turn, with the children.

BE POSITIVE WITH, AND SUPPORTIVE OF, YOUR HUSBAND, BUT ALSO HONOR YOUR OWN POSITION.

This is not possible without true love for your partner. Let's say you marry a man for the social position. Or you want a child, and you want a handsome, intelligent man to be the father. You can talk yourself into anything. But the only thing you're going to be left with—or not—is the deeper connection. You have to honor your man. And then, he honors you. That's a marvelous feeling, isn't it? It feels complete. And your stepchildren will not have access to that space. That's where the door closes to their manipulations.

> "Your soul is oftentimes a battlefield, upon
> which your reason and your judgement wage
> war against your passion and your appetite."
>
> ∾ KG

Do not volunteer your "wisdom" about his children to your husband.

"He who seeks ecstasy in love should not complain of suffering."

∾ KG

This step seems to speak for itself . . . but it takes concentration and conviction to achieve the kind of confidence that allows you to manage your dual role without chronic objection. Your husband may have guilt about his children—remember that his remorse, and his emotional involvement with them, have nothing to do with you, and you must be prepared to deal with his inability to see the problem or hear about its effect on you. If your husband still has a relationship with the mother of his children, he may be dealing with issues of broken commitments, jealousy, and the continued attachments that are an inescapable result of their history as a couple and as parents. There will be times in which your criticism is warranted—but first, step back and take a good look at the bigger picture. Stop and ask yourself, "Is *this* the mountain I want to die on?"

DO NOT BE TOO INTIMATE WITH YOUR HUSBAND
IN FRONT OF HIS CHILDREN.

Your husband is your primary relationship; keep
your bond sacred. Create a place for the two of you
that the children cannot enter, where you and he can
refresh and fortify your marriage for the inevitable
challenges brought by every other aspect of life.

> "The problem with marriage is that it ends every
> night after making love, and it must be rebuilt
> every morning before breakfast."
>
> ❧ GABRIEL GARCÍA MÁRQUEZ

7

The Steps to Take in
Your Relationship with
Your Stepchildren

IN EVERY CIRCUMSTANCE BETWEEN YOU AND
YOUR STEPCHILDREN, TAKE A GOOD LOOK AT YOUR
OWN MOTIVATIONS.

"It is when your spirit goes wandering upon the
wind,
That you, alone and unguarded, commit a wrong
unto others and therefore unto yourself."

∾ KG

Step back and take stock of your part in the situation at hand. Are you concerned about the safety of the child? About the quality of their education? Or are you motivated by your own need for control? If you are to be of real service to the child, you have to detach yourself from your need to be "right."

Do not try to please your stepchildren,
or try to get their approval, as they will
think you to be insincere.

> "You are good when you strive to give of yourself.
> Yet you are not evil when you seek gain for
> yourself."
>
> ෴ KG

There are people to whom you can give and give,
and they're never going to give back. They simply
don't find the time to be gracious. This is not how I
was raised. Perhaps my stepchildren would tell you
I'm a stickler for manners, but I was disappointed
if I gave of myself—cooked and served dinner, for
instance—and never heard from them, "How lovely,
how delicious." Instead, I'd receive criticism about
the flavor of the meat, or the dressing on the salad.
However, whenever I hired someone to cater the
meal, they expressed their appreciation easily!

You as the giver have to step back, shift your
expectations. But it's not just stepping back physically. If you think you're being treated as if you don't
exist—like a non-person, I've often said—you have
to step back intellectually and emotionally.

DO NOT TRY TO MAKE THEM ACCEPT YOU. LET
THEIR OWN EMOTIONS BRING THEM TO YOU.

"It is well to give when asked, but it is better to
give unasked, through understanding . . ."

∾ KG

Waiting for them to come to you is a difficult,
sometimes agonizing, feat. But you mustn't crowd
their space with your emotions, or they will feel
controlled instead of loved. Again, expectation is the
killer, the belief that we can somehow change their
minds about us. The child has to change his own
mind, in his own time.

One of my friends told me about an unexpected moment that occurred one Saturday morning between her and her little stepdaughter, who'd
turned on the TV in the living room to watch car-
toons before breakfast. Instead of asking her to turn
off the TV to eat in the kitchen, my friend brought
juice and cereal for both of them into the living room,
and watched the cartoon with her stepdaughter.

After finishing her breakfast, the little girl
snuggled up to her stepmother without taking
her eyes off the screen and said, "This is why we're

friends." The now-ancient memory of this simple endearment still warms my friend's heart.

RESIST BEING THEIR TEACHER. RESIST THE URGE TO WANT TO MAKE A DIFFERENCE IN THEIR LIVES.

> "The teacher who walks in the shadow of the
> temple, among his followers, gives not of
> his wisdom but rather of his faith and his
> lovingness.
>   If he is indeed wise he does not bid you
> enter the house of his wisdom, but rather leads
> you to the threshold of your own mind."
>
> ~ KG

"Show, don't tell" is a more effective strategy than we realize. We teach more effectively through modeling than through words. A child observes our behavior without comprehending its motivation, but it will resonate and manifest in their lives sooner or later.

So, forget the words—but if you do need to use words, put them in the form of a question. You're the adult, so they will expect you to tell them your opinion, to give your advice, to judge them. Instead, ask them to help you understand. In this situation, the best thing you can give them is the benefit of the doubt.

OFFER YOUR ADVICE ONLY WHEN ASKED.

> "You talk when you cease to be at peace with
>   your thoughts;
> And when you can no longer dwell in the
>   solitude of your heart you live in your lips,
>   and sound is a diversion and a pastime."
>
>   ∽ KG

Your stepchildren will resist your guidance as a matter of course . . . so, try to keep your judgements to yourself. When asked for your help, find an unrelated example or tell a story that addresses their question; let them be the decision makers. This gives them a chance to come to their own conclusion—and makes it difficult for them to perceive you as "judgemental."

DO NOT HAVE TOO MANY EXPECTATIONS ABOUT
THE GIFTS YOU GIVE TO YOUR STEPCHILDREN.
YOUR EFFORTS ARE NOT LIKELY TO BE
APPRECIATED, AND YOU WILL BE DEPRIVED OF THE
PLEASURE OF GIVING.

> "There are those who give little of the much
> > which they have and they give it for
> > recognition and their hidden desire makes
> > their gifts unwholesome.
> And there are those who have little and give it
> > all.
> These are the believers in life and the bounty of
> > life, and their coffer is never empty.
> There are those who give with joy, and that joy
> > is their reward.
> And there are those who give with pain, and
> > that pain is their baptism."

∾ KG

One Christmas, I gave my teenaged stepdaughter a
gift that came in a giant box. The very size of the
box made her excited to open it, regardless of what
was inside—which heightened my excitement about
giving the gift to her!

It doesn't matter now what it was—I simply enjoyed the big smile and the warm hug she gave me after she unwrapped the present. I'd put much time and thought into finding a gift that would please my stepdaughter, who was, truth be told, rather hard to please.

She put on a good show . . . but I never once saw the gift in use, nor did I ever hear it mentioned after that day.

I cannot blame her for not fulfilling my expectations. I am responsible for my disappointment, with the self-manufactured thoughts of victory and validation that, in the last analysis, mean nothing.

ENCOURAGE COMFORTABLE CONVERSATIONS ABOUT YOUR STEPCHILDREN'S PAST, AND THEIR LIVES WITH THEIR MOTHER. ALLOW THEM TO FEEL SAFE TALKING ABOUT THEIR MOTHER IN YOUR COMPANY.

Remember, though, that this is an intimacy they may not want to share with you. In their minds, this would elevate you, the stepmother, in an emotional way that might be seen as crossing over into their mother's "territory." Stepchildren have a need to uphold their mother, to keep her in a very special place, to protect her. You may think they are trying to protect her from you—but it is really that they want to protect her for themselves.

> "We don't set out to save the world; we set out to wonder how other people are doing and to reflect on how our actions affect other people's hearts."
>
> ~ PEMA CHODRON

DO NOT CRITICIZE. DO NOT COMPARE ONE CHILD TO ANOTHER.

I realize I'd do this when I wanted to hurt one of my stepchildren, as a retaliation for the pain they caused me. "You're just like your sister." That was my manipulation. Nobody wants to be "just like." Don't do it.

> "Comparison is the death of joy."
>
> ~ MARK TWAIN

As with giving advice, this is an instance in which you can make your point by telling a story about someone else and hope that it will fall on open ears.

The children will hear you more clearly if you don't make it personal. When you use someone else as a point of reference, it's easier for them to hear and accept the criticism.

ESTABLISH VERY FEW RULES; BUT CLEARLY SPELL OUT THE RULES YOU DO MAKE, TO PREVENT CONFRONTATIONS.

You and your husband know what you will and won't tolerate. Discuss the rules you both create, make an agreement between everyone involved, and stick to the agreement. Make the consequences of their actions very clear.

For me, it's inconsiderate for a child to come late to dinner, or be improperly dressed, or bring their phone to the table. At one dinner, we adults set the table while the kids were watching television. Before dinner, I let the children know we would not eat until their father was seated at the table. This rule worked for awhile. But a new rule needed to be established when one child or the other would find a way to get away from the dinner table by saying they had to go to the bathroom. Children were up and down through the entire meal! I said to all of them, "From now on, we will all go to the bathroom before dinner starts—that way, we won't be getting up in the middle of the meal." I imagined they were secretly rolling their eyes at me, but my preference was now the law of the table.

At another dinner gathering a few months later, my stepdaughter came to the table and immediately began eating. My stepson watched his sister for a few seconds, then said, "Dad is not at the table . . . you know we shouldn't eat, yet!" I was delighted that my stepson remembered the rule—even if my stepdaughter didn't!

DO NOT LET ANY SITUATION WITH YOUR STEPCHILDREN BECOME PERSONAL.

Keep the focus on what happened, and not on how the incident affected you. Take your feelings out of the equation, and acknowledge the feelings of the stepchild.

My friend's stepson had been instructed to improve his math skills, and my friend offered to help. He'd bring her his math problems, and she'd check his progress, making suggestions along the way. A few months later, her "student" told her that his teacher wanted to meet the person who helped him understand the problems he'd been given. My friend was, of course, delighted that she had even the slightest positive effect on her stepson's schoolwork.

But almost immediately, she detected a change in the climate whenever her stepson's mother would drop him off at the house, or pick him up.

Now, her stepson would refrain from hugging my friend when the mother came into view. The child would quickly disconnect from her, which made her sad. She realized she had to step back, to make an inner shift from sorrow to the realization that whatever jealousy the mother was feeling had nothing to do with her.

8

The Steps to Take in Your Relationship with Your Family

NEVER SPEAK NEGATIVELY ABOUT THE MOTHER, EVEN IF IT MIGHT BE DESERVED.

> "Compassion is not a relationship between the healer and the wounded. It's a relationship between equals. Only when we know our own darkness well can we be present with the darkness of others. Compassion becomes real when we recognize our shared humanity."
>
> ❧ PEMA CHODRON

My stepson was 14, and as the only boy (the youngest after three girls), he was the prince of the family. My husband and I had made plans to have lunch with him, and when we called at noon, his mother said, "Lunch isn't going to work. He's still sleeping, and he needs his sleep." This lack of consideration for our plans was an indication to me of how the boy was being raised; the mother wasn't allowing her son to keep his agreement with us. I thought she was setting a poor example for him, but I kept that thought to myself, knowing that making such an observation would serve no positive purpose.

BE AWARE OF NOT GETTING INTO A COMPETITION WITH YOUR STEPCHILDREN FOR THE AFFECTION OR ATTENTION OF YOUR HUSBAND AND THEIR FATHER.

My first husband wasn't aware of it, but his son had gotten into the habit of hounding me, fighting to be the top dog with his father. One weekend when my first stepson was staying with us, my husband was out of the house, and my stepson started in, casting aspersions on my homemaking and lobbing little threats. "By the way," he said as we crossed paths in the kitchen, "You need to get more milk. You don't want my father to find out I did not have any milk, or you'll be in trouble." It made me angry, and when my husband got home, I let him know about it. The fact that it caused an argument between us seems silly now, but it was only one of many instances in which a stepchild had vied for his father's attention by trying to drive a wedge between me and my husband.

"Take someone who doesn't keep score, who's
not looking to be richer, or afraid of losing, who
has not the slightest interest even in his own
personality: he's free."

                 ∾ Rumi

Try not to have disagreements with your husband in front of the children.

Your stepchildren will interpret any disharmony
exhibited by you and your husband as a weakness
in your relationship, and may use these arguments
to stir the pot, creating situations that force your
husband/their father to take sides.

"Would that I could be the peacemaker in
your soul, that I might turn the discord and
the rivalry of your elements into oneness and
melody.
     But how shall I, unless you yourselves be
also the peacemakers, nay, the lovers of all your
elements?"

                 ∾ KG

ENCOURAGE A HEALTHY, HAPPY RELATIONSHIP
BETWEEN THE CHILDREN AND THEIR FATHER.

Nurture trust between the father and his children.
Create comfortable settings for interactions between
them. Create private times between the father and
his children, without your presence. Then, step back
and allow them to have their time together.

> "To have faith is to trust yourself in the water.
> When you swim, you don't grab hold of the
> water, because if you do, you will sink and
> drown. Instead, you relax and float."
>
> ∾ ALAN WATTS

DO NOT HAVE EXPECTATIONS OF SUPPORT FROM
THEIR FATHER WHEN YOU HAVE AN ISSUE WITH
HIS CHILDREN.

My first husband's daughter was living in New
York and came to stay with us in Los Angeles for
a few days. In the middle of her visit with us, she
wanted to leave and stay overnight with a boy who
was traveling through town—and they'd be staying
in the boy's hotel room. I thought it was terribly

disrespectful, and I told her so. She was offended; she reminded me that she was 23, she lived in New York . . . and, "I can do what I want!"

I held my ground, and she left. After she walked out the door, my husband shot me a look that told me he was definitely not pleased.

"You're not dealing with a child," he snapped.

"But this is her father's house, and she leaves with a toothbrush to be with a guy who's just passing through town!"

He did not agree with my opinion, and we argued for two hours—at the end of which, I still felt I was right.

A short time after our blowup quieted, the doorbell rang. I opened the door to my weeping stepdaughter, who said, "You know, this is the first time that somebody really cared about me." It wasn't just the door that opened; it was her heart.

This was one of the most gratifying moments I've had as a stepmother—not because I was right, but because I connected with my stepdaughter, woman-to-woman.

"Happiness doesn't always come from a pursuit. Sometimes it comes when we least expect it."

                 ∾ DALAI LAMA XIV

ENGAGE THE FATHER'S INVOLVEMENT.

"Fathers are biological necessities, but social
accidents."

∾ MARGARET MEAD

I've said that my first husband preferred to behave
like an uncle with his children, instead of a father
who shares every responsibility (which certainly
includes the discipline of his children). A friend of
mine had a similar issue with her husband, who saw
his daughter every other weekend, and took great
care to make those comparatively rare visits festive.
My friend's frustration with her husband was similar to mine with my husband: she saw that he was
being more of an occasional playmate than a father
to his child, and their bond had to be rewoven every
time they got together. A large part of the problem
may well have been the infrequency of the daughter's visits—but that was a negotiation between the
child's parents over which my friend had no control.

    She decided to help her husband be less of a
"friend" and more of a father by suggesting they
both fully integrate the girl into their home and
their lives, as opposed to treating her like a special
visitor. Instead of taking a trip to Disneyland or

going on an exclusive toy shopping excursion, they stayed home and played board games, shopped for food and cooked meals together, took walks around the neighborhood, talked, connected. Before, when his daughter stayed on the phone with a friend after she'd been called to dinner, it was up to the stepmother to be the "bad guy." After the father and daughter bonded, and they became more comfortable together, the father had more authority . . . and used it, while the stepmother stepped back and smiled.

9

What's *Your* Story?

have always enjoyed creating festive Christmas parties for family and friends, filling the house with a warm ambience, beautiful decor and delicious food. In my first marriage, I hosted many Christmas Eves with my husband, inviting his four children, his mother (who wasn't one of my biggest fans), and a small group of close friends. After every party, I always felt let down. Each year, my stepchildren arrived, ate quickly, received gifts perfunctorily and, with a polite thank-you, departed—all within a fraction of the time it took me to plan and prepare the party. I never received from any of them a day-after thanks for the evening, which I thought terribly impolite. But my husband would excuse them every year, coming up with different reasons for each of them—which didn't really make me feel any better.

One Christmas, I developed an acute case of laryngitis the day before the party—I completely lost my voice! I briefly thought about canceling the evening, but we decided to carry on. I crafted a big sign to flash at my guests: "I have laryngitis and cannot speak. Merry Christmas!"

The party went off without any other hitches, and it seemed not to be the flop I thought it might be, since I wasn't able to engage vocally. I'd successfully protected my voice and fêted my family—a surprising feat for me!

The bigger surprise, however, came the next day: every one of the children called to thank me for the delightful Christmas Eve party! After the last call had come, I asked my husband what he thought had gotten into his kids. My husband flashed me a warm smile and said, "You *must* be aware of the big difference between last night's party and all the others you've thrown." I couldn't think of a thing—it was, essentially, the same event I designed every year. "Are you forgetting that you could not speak a word to anyone all evening?"

It took me a moment to realize the difference my forced silence had made in the holiday proceedings. I'd unwittingly given my guests—especially my stepchildren—an opportunity to be themselves, and to relate to their father without my input or influence. I'd always been under the impression that what I had to say was positive, and in their best interest. Obviously, I was mistaken. And it was a valuable lesson for me.

Losing my voice compelled me to step back—and the dividend was significant.

—o—

Of course, I am not suggesting that chronic laryngitis will cure all the difficulties you'll encounter as a stepmother! On the contrary; your voice is incredibly important when used with good judgement and positive intentions. One of the most productive ways to use your voice is by speaking with, and listening to, other stepmothers.

One of my friends became a stepmother early in her life, and had no stepmothers with whom she could commiserate (this was before the Internet made connectivity so incredibly easy). Every woman she knew, whether they were family or friends, were birth mothers, or grandmothers, or not mothers. With no one in her life to offer their guidance or advice from experience or observation, she often thought she was failing as a stepmother. "But," she said to me recently, "how could I be considered a failure when I chose a man with a child from a broken relationship? I had come into a situation that had already failed; did I think I could 'fix' it? Was I expected to 'fix' it?" She isn't the only stepmother in the world who has thought those thoughts or felt those feelings.

She didn't have the resources you now have to reach out in your community and find each other. You can make time to meet, in person or on the phone, and talk. Compare notes and thoughts, to bring and receive the wisdom we all develop when we are challenged by life. Grassroots support groups have served individuals for years, helping them to become stronger in their lives by sharing their stories and receiving encouragement from their fellows. If we can remove the stigma of alcoholism, drug addiction and sexual assault through collective support, we can certainly reframe the notion of stepmothers as "stepmonsters" by telling our stories, sharing our expectations and experiences. We'll become stronger women, better partners to our husbands, and (very possibly) more effective stepmothers to our inherited children.

—o—

A stepmother's world is not the stuff of fairytales. She fights just as hard as any mother—perhaps sometimes a little harder—to love her man, to accept his children, to create a harmonious home. One whose true heart has led her to the complexity of this life should not be treated like an evil witch, but respected like a good woman.

ACKNOWLEDGEMENTS

With thanks to all who have inspired and encouraged me . . . particularly these four women:

My editor, Alexandra Barnes Leh, for bringing her years of editorial expertise and life experience to the sculpting of this book . . .

Jolie Godoy, whose composure under pressure, and whose ability to find symmetry in disarray, never fail to impress me . . .

Lynn Berger, my dear friend and confidante of 40 years . . .

Vicki Reynolds, my wise and valued ally . . .

And to my stepchildren, without whom I would not have achieved so much self-awareness.

ABOUT THE AUTHOR

MARGIT BERNARD was born in Czechoslovakia; her comfortable childhood was interrupted when she became a refugee during the Russian occupation of her country in World War II. She has been a fashion model in London, a business owner in Los Angeles, and a corporate administrator in Paris. Ms. Bernard has a degree in Psychology from USC and serves on the Board of Directors of The Cotsen Foundation for The Art of Teaching.

Ms. Bernard lives in Los Angeles with her husband and two Labrador Retrievers. She is the stepmother of seven, and stepgrandmother of 17.

CPSIA information can be obtained
at www.ICGtesting.com
Printed in the USA
LVHW050932200120
644155LV00008B/1309